Office of Consumer Financial Protection and Access

Fair Lending Guide

July 2017

National Credit Union Administration Fair Lending Guide

# Table of Contents

Using this Guide .................................................................................................. 2
Introduction ......................................................................................................... 3

**Equal Credit Opportunity Act (Regulation B)**
Overview .............................................................................................................. 6
Operational Requirements ................................................................................. 9
Review Considerations ..................................................................................... 12
Checklist ............................................................................................................ 18
Definitions ......................................................................................................... 24

**Fair Housing Act**
Overview ............................................................................................................ 29
Operational Requirements ............................................................................... 32
Review Considerations ..................................................................................... 33
Checklist ............................................................................................................ 37
Definitions ......................................................................................................... 38

**Home Mortgage Disclosure Act (Regulation C)**
Overview ............................................................................................................ 40
Operational Requirements ............................................................................... 43
Review Considerations ..................................................................................... 45
Checklist ............................................................................................................ 48
Definitions ......................................................................................................... 51

Office of Consumer Financial Protection and Access
National Credit Union Administration

## Using this Guide

This guide is intended for use by a credit union's board of directors and management, compliance officers, and others having responsibility for fair lending compliance as part of their duties. While the guide covers federal fair lending laws and regulations that affect federal credit unions, it does not address all federal consumer protection laws or any state laws.

This fair lending guide is divided into five sections:

- Overviews – provide a brief description of what is covered in each fair lending law and regulation, what the regulations require of credit unions, and some potential risks.

- Operational requirements – denote specific requirements covered in each fair lending law and regulation and possible administrative actions for noncompliance.

- Review Considerations – contain various areas management should consider when evaluating fair lending compliance issues or developing compliance policies.

- Checklists – can be used to test compliance with the various fair lending laws and regulations, or as a starting point in developing a policy for compliance with the various regulations. The questions are written so that a "yes" answer indicates compliance with the regulation, and a "no" answer indicates a potential problem area

- Definitions – defines terms used in the narrative sections of this guide as well as terms used in each fair lending law and regulation.

While the content of this guide was carefully reviewed for applicability and accuracy, changes occur in the wording and interpretation of consumer compliance regulations. If a situation arises where this guide becomes inconsistent with the provisions of applicable laws or regulations, the requirement of the law or regulation will prevail.

# Introduction

**Overview of Fair Lending Laws and Regulations**

This overview provides a basic and abbreviated discussion of federal fair lending laws and regulations. It is adapted from the Interagency Policy Statement on Fair Lending issued in March 1994.

The Equal Credit Opportunity Act (ECOA) prohibits discrimination in any aspect of a credit transaction. It applies to any extension of credit, including extensions of credit to small businesses, corporations, partnerships, and trusts.
The ECOA prohibits discrimination based on:

- Race or color
- Religion
- National origin
- Sex
- Marital status
- Age (provided the applicant has the capacity to contract)
- The applicant's receipt of income derived from any public assistance program
- The applicant's exercise, in good faith, of any right under the Consumer Credit Protection Act

Regulation B, found at 12 CFR part 1002, implements the ECOA. Regulation B describes lending acts and practices that are specifically prohibited, permitted, or required. Official staff interpretations of the regulation are found in Supplement I to 12 CFR part 1002.

The Fair Housing Act (FH Act) prohibits discrimination in all aspects of "residential real-estate related transactions," including but not limited to:

- Making loans to buy, build, repair or improve a dwelling
- Purchasing real estate loans
- Selling, brokering, or appraising residential real estate
- Selling or renting a dwelling

The FH Act prohibits discrimination based on:

- Race or color
- National origin
- Religion

- Sex
- Familial status (defined as children under the age of 18 living with a parent or legal custodian, pregnant women, and people securing custody of children under 18)
- Handicap

U.S. Department of Housing and Urban Development (HUD) regulations implementing the FH Act are found at 24 CFR Part 100. Because both the FH Act and the ECOA apply to mortgage lending, lenders may not discriminate in mortgage lending based on any of the prohibited factors in either list.

Under the ECOA, it is unlawful for a lender to discriminate on a prohibited basis in any aspect of a credit transaction, and under both the ECOA and the FH Act, it is unlawful for a lender to discriminate on a prohibited basis in a residential real-estate-related transaction. Under one or both of these laws, a lender may not, because of a prohibited factor:

- Fail to provide information or services or provide different information or services regarding any aspect of the lending process, including credit availability, application procedures, or lending standards
- Discourage or selectively encourage applicants with respect to inquiries about or applications for credit
- Refuse to extend credit or use different standards in determining whether to extend credit
- Vary the terms of credit offered, including the amount, interest rate, duration, or type of loan
- Use different standards to evaluate collateral
- Treat a borrower differently in servicing a loan or invoking default remedies
- Use different standards for pooling or packaging a loan in the secondary market.

A lender may not express, orally or in writing, a preference based on prohibited factors or indicate that it will treat applicants differently on a prohibited basis. A violation may still exist even if a lender treated applicants equally.

A lender may not discriminate on a prohibited basis because of the characteristics of:

- An applicant, prospective applicant, or borrower
- A person associated with an applicant, prospective applicant, or borrower (for example, a co-applicant, spouse, business partner, or live-in aide)
- The present or prospective occupants of either the property to be financed or the characteristics of the neighborhood or other area where property to be financed is located.

Finally, the FH Act requires lenders to make reasonable accommodations for a person with disabilities when such accommodations are necessary to afford the person an equal opportunity to apply for credit.

**National Credit Union Administration (NCUA) Enforcement of Fair Lending Laws**

NCUA implemented its fair lending examination program in 1999. With the exception of those federally insured credit unions with assets over $10 billion, which are under the authority of the Consumer Financial Protection Bureau, NCUA enforces ECOA and Regulation B in federal credit unions and the Home Mortgage Disclosure Act (HMDA) and Regulation C in all federally insured credit unions.

ECOA requires NCUA to refer matters to the U.S. Department of Justice (DOJ) when NCUA has a reason to believe that a federal credit union has engaged in a pattern or practice of discrimination on a prohibited basis. NCUA's fair lending examination program also assesses compliance with the FH Act, but HUD and DOJ enforce the FH Act. NCUA reports violations of the FH Act to HUD or DOJ. NCUA conducts fair lending examinations at and supervisory contacts with federal credit unions to assess compliance with fair lending laws using the Federal Financial Institutions Examination Council (FFIEC) Interagency Fair Lending Examination Procedures (August 2009).

Office of Consumer Financial Protection and Access
National Credit Union Administration

# EQUAL CREDIT OPPORTUNITY ACT (REGULATION B) OVERVIEW

The Equal Credit Opportunity Act (ECOA), implemented by Regulation B (12 CFR 1002), promotes availability of credit to all creditworthy applicants without regard to race, color, religion, national origin, sex, marital status, age (provided the applicant has the capacity to contract), receipt of public assistance, or good faith exercise of any rights under the Consumer Credit Protection Act.

The basic rule of Regulation B, as found in §1002.4, is:
*"A creditor shall not discriminate against any applicant on a prohibited basis with respect to any aspect of a credit transaction."*

Prohibited basis refers not only to the characteristics of the applicant, but also to the characteristics of individuals with whom the applicant is affiliated or associates. Therefore, a credit union may not discriminate against a member-applicant based on a prohibited basis characteristic of an associated individual. For example, a credit union cannot discriminate against an applicant because of the race of the residents in the neighborhood where the collateral property is located.

Credit transaction means every aspect of an applicant's dealings with a credit union regarding an application for credit or an existing extension of credit including, but not limited to, information requirements, investigation procedures, standards of creditworthiness, terms of credit, furnishing of credit information, revocation, alteration, or termination of credit, and collection procedures.

Regulation B also requires credit unions to do the following:

- Notify applicants of the credit decision within 30 days of receiving a completed application.
- Retain records of credit applications for 25 months after notifying the member of its credit decision.
- Collect information about the applicant's race and other personal characteristics in applications for certain dwelling-related loans.
- Provide applicants with copies of appraisal reports used in connection with credit transactions.

**Credit Applications**

Regulation B prevents credit unions from discouraging prospective applicants from making or pursuing an application.

Credit unions are encouraged to use industry standard form applications. A credit union choosing to use a non-standard credit application form should obtain a legal opinion stating the forms comply with the applicable legal requirements.
The application may request any information, <u>except</u> for information about the member's:

- Spouse, unless the spouse will use or is contractually liable on the account or the applicant relies on the spouse's income
- Marital status when applying for unsecured credit when applying for secured credit, the application may use only the terms married, unmarried, or separated
- Sex, race, color, religion, and national origin
- Childrearing or childbearing, such as birth control practices, intentions, or capability to bear children

A credit union may consider any information obtained in the credit application provided it does not use the information to discriminate against an applicant on a prohibited basis. An exception to this rule relates to the consideration of age in determining an applicant's creditworthiness.

**Self-Test for Compliance**

On April 15, 2003, Regulation B was amended to address the collection of applicants' personal characteristics in connection with non-mortgage credit. The mandatory compliance date was April 15, 2004.

This exception allows creditors to collect personal characteristics in a self-test for compliance with the ECOA in order to allow creditors to develop compliance programs that utilize applicant data in a controlled and targeted manner. A self-test is a program, practice, or study designed and used by a creditor specifically to determine compliance with the ECOA. The creditor must take corrective action when the results of the self-test indicate that "it is more likely than not" that a violation occurred.

Creditors that conduct a self-test and request information about personal characteristics must disclose to applicants that:

- Providing the information is optional
- It is being collected to monitor for compliance with the ECOA
- It will not be used in making the credit decision
- If applicable, information may be noted based on visual observation or surname

**Effects Test**

While not specifically mentioned in the ECOA, the legislative history of the ECOA indicates Congress intended an "effects test" concept to apply to a credit union's determination of creditworthiness. The effects test refers to a credit practice that appears facially neutral, but has a disproportionately negative effect on a prohibited basis, even though the credit union has no intent to discriminate. This type of practice is discriminatory, in effect, unless the credit union can demonstrate the practice meets a legitimate business need that cannot be reasonably achieved by means less disparate in impact.

Answering the following questions should assist in determining if the credit union's credit practices result in a potential violation of the effects test:

1. Does a particular credit practice have a statistically disproportionate impact on a protected group (those covered under the prohibited basis definition)?
2. If so, can the credit union show that the practice serves a genuine business need?
3. If so, is there a less discriminating way to meet that business need?

**Appraisals**

Currently, federal credit unions are subject to the appraisal requirements outlined in Section 701.31(c)(5) and Part 722 of the NCUA Rules and Regulations.

Effective January 18, 2014, federal credit unions will be subject to Section 1002.14 (Rules on providing appraisals and other valuations) of Regulation B. Refer to Operational Requirements section for more information.

**Associated Risks**

- Compliance risk can occur when the credit union fails to implement the necessary controls to comply with the ECOA.
- Reputation risk can occur when the credit union incurs fines and penalties or receives negative publicity or declined membership confidence as a result of failure to comply with ECOA.

**Additional Information**

The Consumer Financial Protection Bureau's website contains additional information at http://www.consumerfinance.gov/.

Please note the ECOA and the Fair Housing Act should be read together in order to fully understand the scope of a credit union's fair lending obligations.

# EQUAL CREDIT OPPORTUNITY ACT (REGULATION B) OPERATIONAL REQUIREMENTS

**Disclosures / Notices**

Appraisal Reports [Section 1002.14]

Effective January 18, 2014, Section 1002.14 will:

- Require creditors to notify applicants within three business days of receiving an application of their right to receive a copy of appraisals developed.
- Require creditors to provide applicants a copy of each appraisal and other written valuation promptly upon their completion or three business days before consummation (for closed-end credit) or account opening (for open-end credit), whichever is earlier.
- Permit applicants to waive the timing requirement for providing these copies. However, applicants who waive the timing requirement must be given a copy of all appraisals and other written valuations at or prior to consummation or account opening, or if the transaction is not consummated or the account is not opened, no later than 30 days after the creditor determines the transaction will not be consummated or the account will not be opened.
- Prohibit creditors from charging for the copy of appraisals and other written valuations, but permits creditors to charge applicants reasonable fees for the cost of the appraisals or other written valuation unless applicable law provides otherwise.

Notification of Action Taken [Section 1002.9(a)]

The creditor must notify an applicant of the action taken on a credit application, in accordance with the requirements of Section 1002.9. The notification must be in writing and must include a statement of the action taken, the name and address of the creditor, a statement of the provisions of Section 701(a) of the ECOA (see Section 1002.9(b)), the name and address of the creditor's federal regulator, and a statement of the specific reasons for the action or the disclosure of the right to obtain such reasons. Generally, the notice must be provided within 30 days after receipt of a completed application. The notification requirements for business credit applicants may vary somewhat as described in Section 1002.9(a)(3).

ECOA Notice [Section 1002.9(b)]

When providing a notification of action taken in connection with the requirements of Section 1002.9(a), the creditor must provide a statement of the provisions of Section 701(a) of the ECOA that is substantially similar to the language contained in Section 1002.9(b).

Monitoring Information [Section 1002.13]

A creditor must inform applicant(s) for a home mortgage loan that the federal government requests information on ethnicity, race, sex, marital status, and age for monitoring purposes. The creditor must also inform the applicant(s) that if they choose not to provide the information, the creditor is required to note the ethnicity, race, and sex on the basis of visual observation or surname.

Equal Housing Lender Poster [NCUA Rules and Regulations Sections 701.31(d)(2)]

Federal credit unions engaging in real estate-related lending must display a notice of nondiscrimination. The notice (with the prescribed logo and language) must be placed in the public lobby of the credit union and in the public areas of each office where such loans are made and must be clearly visible to the general public.

**Written Programs / Documentation**

Written Applications [Section 1002.4(c)]

A creditor must take written applications for the types of credit covered by Section 1002.13(a), i.e., applications for credit related to the purchase or refinancing of a principal residence secured by the residence.

**Recordkeeping**

Record Retention [Section 1002.12]

Applications, supporting information, and required notifications generally must be retained for 25 months (12 months for business credit) from the date of the notice of action taken. A longer retention period may apply if an investigation or enforcement proceeding is underway.

Creditors must retain for 25 months certain records related to prescreened solicitations, such as the list of criteria used to select potential customers.

**Advertising**

No Discouraging Applications on a Prohibited Basis [Section 1002.4(b)]

A credit union must not make any oral or written statement that discourages applicants or prospective applicants on a prohibited basis from making or pursuing an application.

Nondiscriminatory Advertising [NCUA Rules and Regulations Section 701.31(d)]

No federal credit union may engage in any form of advertising of real estate-related loans that indicates the credit union discriminates on a prohibited basis. Advertisements must not contain any words, symbols, models, or other forms of communication that suggest a discriminatory preference or policy of exclusion.

Advertisements of real estate products must include a facsimile of the prescribed equal housing lender logo (for written advertisements) or prescribed language (for oral advertisements).

**Reports**

Reporting Credit Information [Section 1002.10]

If a credit union reports credit information to a consumer reporting agency or in response to a credit inquiry, and the account reflects the participation of both spouses, the credit union must furnish the information in a manner that enables access to or provides the information for the particular spouse in question.

**Enforcement / Liability**

Administrative Enforcement Authority [Section 704 of the ECOA]

The Consumer Financial Protection Bureau has responsibility for enforcement at credit unions with greater than $10 billion in assets. The National Credit Union Administration has responsibility for enforcement at federal credit unions with less than $10 billion in assets. The Federal Trade Commission enforces Regulation B at state-chartered credit unions with less than $10 billion in assets.

Penalties and Liabilities [Section 1002.16(b)]

Regulation B provides for actual damages, as well as for punitive damages of up to $10,000 in individual lawsuits and up to the lesser of $500,000 or one percent of the institution's net worth in class action suits. Court costs and reasonable attorney fees may also be awarded to an aggrieved applicant in a successful action.

Office of Consumer Financial Protection and Access
National Credit Union Administration

# EQUAL CREDIT OPPORTUNITY ACT (REGULATION B) REVIEW CONSIDERATIONS

All reviews need not be full-scope but may be focused to the areas posing the most risk to the credit union.

| Review Area | Requirements / Recommendations |
| --- | --- |
| Policies / Procedures | Ensure the policy for implementing ECOA (Regulation B) does not tolerate discrimination in any aspect of the credit transaction process. |
| No Discrimination on a Prohibited Basis | Ensure employees do not discriminate on a prohibited basis regarding any aspect of a credit transaction. Prohibited bases: race, color, religion, national origin, sex, marital status, age (provided the applicant has capacity to contract), receipt of public assistance, or exercise of rights under the Consumer Credit Protection Act. |
| No Discouraging of Applications | Ensure employees do not discourage applicants or prospective applicants on a prohibited basis from making or pursuing an application. |
| Inquiries Concerning a Spouse | Ensure employees do not request information concerning the spouse or former spouse except when the spouse has rights of access to the account, is liable on the account, or the applicant is relying on spousal income, support, or property as a basis for repayment. |
| Inquiries Concerning Marital Status | Ensure employees do not inquire about the marital status of an applicant who is applying for individual unsecured credit. For applicants residing in a community property state or relying on property located in such a state, limit applicant marital status information to the categories: married, unmarried, and separated. |
| Inquiries Concerning Other Income | Ensure employees do not inquire whether income stated in application is derived from alimony, child support, or separate |

| | |
|---|---|
| | maintenance payments unless applicant is given a choice as to whether such information is to be considered in the determination of creditworthiness. |
| Inquiries Concerning Applicant's Sex | Ensure employees do not inquire about the applicant's sex; however, an applicant can be requested to designate a title (such as Ms., Miss, Mr., or Mrs.), if the form discloses that such a designation is optional. |
| Inquiries on Childbearing, Childrearing | Ensure employees do not inquire about childbearing or rearing or about birth control practices. Information about dependents may be requested if sought from all applicants. |
| Written Applications | Written applications must be taken for credit related to the purchase or refinancing of a principal residence secured by the residence.<br>(Note: these are the same types of credit for which monitoring information must be collected.) |
| Rules on Use of Information | Creditors are not permitted to take the following into account when evaluating an applicant's creditworthiness:<br><br>1. Any prohibited basis, except as provided by the ECOA and Regulation B;<br>2. Age or receipt of public assistance (with exceptions noted in Section 1002.6(b)(2));<br>3. Assumptions or statistics related to childbearing or childrearing; or<br>4. Telephone listing in name of applicant.<br><br>Also note the following limits on the use of information:<br><br>1. Income – no discounting/exclusion of income if derived from part-time employment, annuity, pension, public assistance, alimony, or child support.<br>2. Credit History – consider accounts that |

| | |
|---|---|
| | the applicant and the applicant's spouse use or on which they are contractually liable. Also consider information offered by applicants concerning inaccuracies in their credit history.<br>3. Immigrant Status – may consider applicant's immigration status as it relates to rights/remedies regarding repayment. |
| Credit Scoring Systems: Use of Age | Use of a credit scoring system that scores age as a predictive variable is permissible only when it is empirically derived and is demonstrably and statistically sound. The age of an elderly applicant may not be assigned a negative factor or value. |
| Self-test | Use information gathered in a controlled and targeted manner to specifically determine compliance with the ECOA.<br><br>The following must be disclosed to applicants:<br><br>• Providing the information is optional.<br>• It is being collected to monitor for compliance with the ECOA.<br>• It will not be used in making the credit decision.<br>• If applicable, information may be noted based on visual observation or surname. |
| Action on Open-End Accounts | Creditors are restricted from terminating, changing account terms, or requiring reapplications for open-end accounts on the basis of changes of age or retirement status. Reapplications may not be required for a change of marital status (where spouse had no liability and spousal income had no impact on credit decision). |
| Spousal Signatures | Creditors are restricted from requiring the signature of an applicant's spouse or other person on any credit instrument if the applicant qualifies for the amount and terms of credit requested. |

| | |
|---|---|
| Insurance | Creditors may not refuse to extend credit and may not terminate an account because credit life, health, accident, disability, or other credit-related insurance is not available based on the applicant's age. |
| Furnishing Credit Information | Creditors reporting credit information must abide by requirements enabling separate tracking of spouses and their individual and/or joint credit histories. |
| Providing Appraisals | Currently, federal credit unions are subject to the appraisal requirements outlined in Section 701.31(c)(5) and Part 722 of the NCUA Rules and Regulations.<br><br>Effective January 18, 2014, federal credit unions will be subject to Section 1002.14 (Rules on providing appraisals and other valuations) of Regulation B. Refer to Operational Requirements for more information. |
| Notification of Action Taken | Creditors must provide written notice of action taken on credit applications that include a statement of specific reasons for the action (or disclosure of right to obtain such reasons), name and address of creditor, and name and address of creditor's federal regulatory agency. The notice must also contain a statement of the provisions of Section 1002.9(b).<br><br>There are special provisions concerning:<br><br>- Notification to business credit applicants (Section 1002.9(a)(3))<br>- Incomplete applications (Section 1002.9(c))<br>- Applications submitted through a third party (Section 1002.9(g)) |
| Monitoring Information | In connection with applications for the purchase or refinancing of a principal residence secured by the residence, the application must request information |

|  |  |
|---|---|
|  | regarding the applicant(s) ethnicity, race, sex, marital status, and age.<br><br>If the applicant(s) chooses not to provide some or all of the information, the creditor should note that fact and, to the extent possible, should also note the ethnicity, race, and sex of the applicant(s) based on visual observation or surname.<br><br>See also additional information that must be disclosed to applicants concerning the collection and use of the monitoring information. (Section 1002.13(c).) |
| Record Retention | • Preserve applications, monitoring information, information used in evaluating the application, and required notifications. Generally, required for 25 months after date of notice of action taken.<br>• Retain records relating to prescreened solicitations for 25 months. |
| Self-Testing | Institutions have a legal privilege in information developed as a result of self-tests that they voluntarily conduct to determine their compliance with the ECOA and Regulation B. The privilege applies only if the definition of self-test is met and the creditor takes appropriate corrective actions as described in Section 1002.15. |
| Training | Provide training to all employees involved in any aspect of taking, evaluating, acting on a credit application, or furnishing/maintaining credit information. In addition, persons involved in marketing and credit operations should receive appropriate instruction relative to their responsibilities. |
| Monitoring, Internal Review, Audit | Monitor the various phases of the credit application process on a periodic basis, including taking and evaluating applications, providing appraisal reports, and reporting credit histories. This process |

|  | should focus on the credit union's compliance with the substantive nondiscrimination requirements as well as its adherence to the technical provisions of the ECOA and Regulation B. |
|  | An internal or external audit should be conducted at least annually to assess overall compliance. |

Office of Consumer Financial Protection and Access
National Credit Union Administration

# EQUAL CREDIT OPPORTUNITY ACT (REGULATION B) CHECKLIST

|  | Yes | No |
|---|---|---|
| 1. Does the credit union prohibit its employees from making statements that would discourage, on a prohibited basis, applicants from making or pursuing an application? [§1002.4(b)] | _____ | _____ |
| 2. Does the credit union refrain from requesting information concerning the applicant's spouse or former spouse unless such person will be permitted to use or be contractually liable, or the applicant is relying on community property, the spouse's income, alimony, child support, or maintenance payments for repayment of the debt? [§1002.5(c)(2)] | _____ | _____ |
| 3. Regarding applications for individual unsecured loans, does the credit union refrain from inquiring as to the marital status of the loan applicant (unless community property is involved)? [§1002.5(d)(1)] | _____ | _____ |
| 4. For secured loans, are inquiries into marital status limited to the terms "married," "unmarried," or "separated?" [§1002.5(d)(1)] | _____ | _____ |
| 5. When income derived from alimony, child support, or maintenance payments is disclosed, is there evidence that the credit union properly informed the applicant that such income need not be revealed? [§1002.5(d)(2)] | _____ | _____ |
| 6. When a title such as Ms., Miss, Mrs., or Mr. is shown on the application, does the form appropriately disclose that such designation is optional? [§1002.5(b)(2)] | _____ | _____ |
| 7. Are requests for information relative to birth control, childbearing, or rearing intentions of applicants prohibited? [§1002.5(d)(3)] | _____ | _____ |

8. If the credit union considers age or the fact that an applicant's income is derived from a public assistance

program, does it do so only to determine a pertinent element of creditworthiness? [§1002.6(b)(2)(iii)]

9. If the age of an elderly applicant is considered, is such age used only to favor the elderly applicant? [§1002.6(b)(2)(iv)]

10. When evaluating the applicant's creditworthiness, does the credit union refrain from considering aggregate statistics or assumptions relative to the likelihood of bearing or rearing children? [§1002.6(b)(3)]

11. Does the credit union refrain from discounting or excluding income on a prohibited basis or because the income is derived from part-time employment, or a retirement benefit? [§1002.6(b)(5)]

12. Does the credit union consider income from alimony, child support, or maintenance payments to the extent it is likely to be consistently received? [§1002.6(b)(5)]

13. When considering an applicant's credit history, does the credit union consider:

a. all accounts designated as accounts that the applicant and applicant's spouse are permitted to use or for which both are contractually liable? [§1002.6(b)(6)(i)]

b. at the applicant's request, any information the applicant may present regarding past credit performance which indicates that such performance does not accurately reflect the applicant's willingness to pay? [§1002.6(b)(6)(ii)]

c. at the applicant's request, any credit information in the name of the applicant's spouse or former spouse which demonstrates the applicant's willingness to pay? [§1002.6(b)(6)(iii)]

14. Does the credit union grant loans to creditworthy applicants regardless of sex, marital status, or membership in any other protected group? [§1002.7(a)]

15. Does the credit union allow the granting of loans in maiden names or combinations of maiden and married names? [§1002.7(b)]

16. When the credit union requires cosigners, is the requirement based on factors other than the applicant's sex, marital status, or other prohibited basis of discrimination? (State law may be considered when determining the necessity for cosigners.)
[Commentary to §1002.7(d)(5)]

17. Are restrictions on spousal signatures observed?
[§1002.7(d)]

18. If a loan can only be approved with a cosigner, could an applicant volunteer any other person and not be limited to a spouse? [§1002.7(d)(5)]

19. Is business credit available separately to principals of corporations, partners, and proprietors without requiring spouses' signatures?
[Commentary to §1002.7(d)(6)]

20. Does the credit union refrain from refusing credit because credit life, health, accident, disability, or other credit-related insurance is not available due to the applicant's age? [§1002.7(e)]

21. Does the credit union notify applicants of action taken within:

a. 30 days of receipt of a completed application?
[§1002.9(a)(1)(i)]

b. 30 days after taking adverse action on an incomplete application? [§1002.9(a)(1)(ii)]

c. 30 days after taking adverse action on an existing account? [§1002.9(a)(1)(iii)]

d. 90 days after notifying the applicant of a counteroffer if the applicant does not expressly accept or use the credit offered? [§1002.9(a)(1)(iv)]

e. a reasonable period, not more than 30 days, after an oral request to complete an incomplete application?
[§1002.9(c)]

22. Are notices of adverse action: [§1002.9(a)(2)]

a. in writing?                                              _____ _____

b. do they contain the name and address of the credit union?   _____ _____

c. do they contain an accurate statement of action taken?   _____ _____

d. do they contain a statement of the provisions of Section 701(a) of the Equal Credit Opportunity Act in a form substantially similar to that contained in §1002.9(b)(1) of the regulation?   _____ _____

e. do they contain the name and address of the credit union's federal regulator?   _____ _____

f. do they contain an accurate statement of specific reasons for the action taken or disclosure of the applicant's right to such a statement as specified in §1002.9(a)(2)?   _____ _____

23. Do statements of specific reasons for adverse action contain the principal, specific reasons for such actions? [§1002.9(b)(2)]   _____ _____

24. Has the credit union established procedures for the identification, and designation as such, of existing and future loans upon which both spouses are or will be contractually liable? [§1002.10(a)]   _____ _____

25. When furnishing credit information on designated accounts to a consumer reporting agency, does the credit union report the designation and furnish the information in a manner that provides access to such information in the name of each spouse? [§1002.10(b)]   _____ _____

26. When furnishing credit information regarding a designated account in response to an inquiry regarding a particular applicant, is the information furnished in the name of such applicant? [§1002.10(c)]   _____ _____

27. Does the credit union retain for 25 months after notice of action taken or notice of incompleteness: [§1002.12(b)]  _____ _____

a. the application and all supporting material?  _____ _____

b. all information obtained for monitoring purposes?  _____ _____

c. the notification of action taken?  _____ _____

d. a statement of specific reasons for adverse action?  _____ _____

e. discrimination complaints under Regulation B?  _____ _____

28. Is all information relative to an investigative action retained until final disposition of the matter? [§1002.12(b)(4)]  _____ _____

29. If the credit union engages in a special purpose credit program, is it in compliance with Section 1002.8 of the Regulation?  _____ _____

30. Has the credit union adopted procedures to comply with notification and record retention requirements on business credit? [§1002.9(a)(3)] and [§1002.12]  _____ _____

31. Does the credit union make available a copy of the appraisal used in connection with the member's real estate-related loan application? [701.31(c)(5), §1002.14 effective January 18, 2014]  _____ _____

32. Does the credit union include in its advertisements of real estate-related loans, that such loans are made without regard to race, color, religion, national origin, sex, handicap, or familial status? [701.31(d)(1)]  _____ _____

33. If the credit union makes real estate-related loans, does it display a notice of nondiscrimination in the public lobby of the credit union and in the public area of each office where such loans are made? [701.31(d)(2)]  _____ _____

34. Does the credit union collect monitoring information (ethnicity, race, sex, marital status, age) as required by §1002.13?  _____ _____

35. If the credit union collects data in a self-test for compliance with the ECOA, does it disclose to the applicants that providing the information is optional, that it is being collected to monitor for compliance with the ECOA, that it will not be used in making the credit decision, and, where applicable, that information may be noted based on visual observation or surname? [§1002.5(b)(1)]  _____  _____

36. Is the self-test designed and used specifically to determine compliance with the ECOA? [§1002.15(b)(1)(i)]  _____  _____

37. Does the credit union retain records related to a self-test for 25 months? [§1002.12(b)(6)]  _____  _____

38. Does the credit union retain records related to prescreened solicitations for 25 months? [§1002.12(b)(7)]  _____  _____

# EQUAL CREDIT OPPORTUNITY ACT (REGULATION B) DEFINITIONS

**Definitions (Section 1002.2)**
For the purposes of Regulation B, unless the context indicates otherwise, the following definitions apply.

### *Account*
An extension of credit. When employed in relation to an account, the word use refers only to open-end credit.

### *Act*
The Equal Credit Opportunity Act (Title VII of the Consumer Credit Protection Act).

### *Adverse action*
(1)(i) a refusal to grant credit in substantially the amount or on substantially the terms requested in an application unless the creditor makes a counteroffer (to grant credit in a different amount or on other terms) and the applicant uses or expressly accepts the credit offered;
(ii) a termination of an account or an unfavorable change in the terms of an account that does not affect all or a substantial portion of a class of the creditor's accounts; or,
(iii) a refusal to increase the amount of credit available to an applicant who has made an application for an increase.

(2) Adverse action does not include:
(i) a change in the terms of an account expressly agreed to by an applicant;
(ii) any action or forbearance relating to an account taken in connection with inactivity, default, or delinquency as to that account;
(iii) a refusal or failure to authorize an account transaction at a point of sale or loan, except when the refusal is a termination or an unfavorable change in the terms of an account that does not affect all or a substantial portion of a class of the creditor's accounts, or when the refusal is a denial of an application for an increase in the amount of credit available under the account;
(iv) a refusal to extend credit because applicable law prohibits the creditor from extending the credit requested; or,
(v) a refusal to extend credit because the creditor does not offer the type of credit or credit plan requested.

(3) An action that falls within the definition of both paragraphs (1) and (2) is governed by
paragraph (2).

### *Age*
Refers only to the age of natural persons and means the number of fully elapsed years from the date of an applicant's birth.

### *Applicant*
Any person who requests or who has received an extension of credit from a creditor, and includes any person who is or may become contractually liable regarding an extension of credit. For purposes of Section 1002.7(d), the term includes guarantors, sureties, endorsers, and similar parties.

### *Application*
An oral or written request for an extension of credit that is made in accordance with procedures established by a creditor for the type of credit requested. The term does not include the use of an account or line of credit to obtain an amount of credit that is within a previously established credit limit. A completed application means an application in connection with which a creditor has received all the information that the creditor regularly obtains and considers in evaluating applications for the amount and type of credit requested (including, but not limited to, credit reports, any additional information requested from the applicant, and any approvals or reports by governmental agencies or other persons that are necessary to guarantee, insure, or provide security for the credit or collateral). The creditor shall exercise reasonable diligence in obtaining such information.

### *Business credit*
Refers to extensions of credit primarily for business or commercial (including agricultural) purposes, but excluding extensions of credit of the types described in Section 1002.3(a), (b), and (d).

### *Consumer credit*
Credit extended to a natural person primarily for personal, family, or household purposes.

### *Contractually liable*
Expressly obligated to repay all debts arising on an account by reason of an agreement to that effect.

### *Credit*
The right granted by a creditor to an applicant to defer payment of a debt, incur debt and defer its payment, or purchase property or services and defer payment therefore.

### *Credit card*
Any card, plate, coupon book, or other single credit device that may be used from time to time to obtain money, property, or services on credit.

### *Creditor*
A person who, in the ordinary course of business, regularly participates in the decision of whether or not to extend credit. The term includes a creditor's assignee, transferee, or subrogee who so participates. For purposes of Sections 1002.4 and 1002.5(a) the term also includes a person who, in the ordinary course of business, regularly refers applicants or prospective applicants to creditors, or selects or offers to select creditors to whom requests for credit may be made. A person is not a creditor regarding any violation of the act or this regulation committed by another creditor unless the person knew or had reasonable notice of the act, policy, or practice that constituted the violation before becoming involved in the credit transaction. The term does not include a person whose only participation in a credit transaction involves honoring a credit card.

### *Credit transaction*
Every aspect of an applicant's dealings with a creditor regarding an application for credit or an existing extension of credit (including, but not limited to, information requirements; investigation procedures; standards of creditworthiness; terms of credit; furnishing of credit information; revocation, alteration, or termination of credit; and collection procedures).

***Discriminate against an applicant*** means to treat an applicant less favorably than other applicants.

### *Elderly*
Age 62 or older.

### *Empirically derived and other credit scoring systems*
(1) A credit scoring system is a system that evaluates an applicant's creditworthiness mechanically, based on key attributes of the applicant and aspects of the transaction, and that determines, alone or in conjunction with an evaluation of additional information about the applicant, whether an applicant is deemed creditworthy. To qualify as an empirically derived, demonstrably and statistically sound, credit scoring system, the system must be:

(i) based on data that are derived from an empirical comparison of sample groups or the population of creditworthy and non-creditworthy applicants who applied for credit within a reasonable preceding period of time;
(ii) developed for the purpose of evaluating the creditworthiness of applicants with respect to the legitimate business interests of the creditor utilizing the system (including, but not limited to, minimizing bad debt losses and operating expenses in accordance with the creditor's business judgment);
(iii) developed and validated using accepted statistical principles and methodology; and,
(iv) periodically revalidated by the use of appropriate statistical principles and methodology and adjusted as necessary to maintain predictive ability.

(2) A creditor may use an empirically derived, demonstrably and statistically sound, credit scoring system obtained from another person or may obtain credit experience from which to develop such a system. Any such system must satisfy the criteria set forth in paragraph (1) (i) through (iv) of this section; if the creditor is unable during the development process to validate the system based on its own credit experience in accordance with paragraph (1) of this section, the system must be validated when sufficient credit experience becomes available. A system that fails this validity test is no longer an empirically derived, demonstrably and statistically sound, credit scoring system for that creditor.

### *Extend credit and extension of credit*
The granting of credit in any form (including, but not limited to, credit granted in addition to any existing credit or credit limit; credit granted pursuant to an open-end credit plan; the refinancing or other renewal of credit, including the issuance of a new credit card in place of an expiring credit card or in substitution for an existing credit card; the consolidation of two or more obligations; or the continuance of existing credit without any special effort to collect at or after maturity).

### *Good faith*
Honesty in fact in the conduct or transaction.

### *Inadvertent error*
A mechanical, electronic, or clerical error that a creditor demonstrates was not intentional and occurred notwithstanding the maintenance of procedures reasonably adapted to avoid such errors.

### *Judgmental system of evaluating applicants*
Any system for evaluating the creditworthiness of an applicant other than an empirically derived, demonstrably and statistically sound, credit scoring system.

### *Marital status*
The state of being unmarried, married, or separated, as defined by applicable state law. The term "unmarried" includes persons who are single, divorced, or widowed.

### *Negative factor or value, in relation to the age of elderly applicants,* means utilizing a factor, value, or weight that is less favorable regarding elderly applicants than the creditor's experience warrants or is less favorable than the factor, value, or weight assigned to the class of applicants that are not classified as elderly and are most favored by a creditor on the basis of age.

### Open-end credit
Credit extended under a plan under which a creditor may permit an applicant to make purchases or obtain loans from time to time directly from the creditor or indirectly by use of a credit card, check, or other device.

### Person
A natural person, corporation, government or governmental subdivision or agency, trust, estate, partnership, cooperative, or association.

### Pertinent element of creditworthiness, in relation to a judgmental system of evaluating
**applicants,** means any information about applicants that a creditor obtains and considers and that has a demonstrable relationship to a determination of creditworthiness.

### Prohibited basis
Race, color, religion, national origin, sex, marital status, or age (provided that the applicant has the capacity to enter into a binding contract); the fact that all or part of the applicant's income derives from any public assistance program; or the fact that the applicant has in good faith exercised any right under the Consumer Credit Protection Act or any state law upon which an exemption has been granted by the Bureau.

### State
Any state, the District of Columbia, the Commonwealth of Puerto Rico, or any territory or possession of the United States.

# FAIR HOUSING ACT OVERVIEW

The Fair Housing Act (FH Act) provides for fair housing throughout the United States. In particular, FH Act makes it unlawful for any lender to discriminate in its housing-related lending activities against any person because of race, color, religion, national origin, sex, handicap, or familial status.

The FH Act works in conjunction with the Equal Credit Opportunity Act (ECOA) to prohibit discrimination by anyone who is in the business of providing loans for housing. The U.S. Department of Housing and Urban Development (HUD) has primary FH Act regulatory and enforcement authority over credit unions. HUD's FH Act regulations are located at 24 CFR Parts 100, 103, and 110, and guidance on discriminatory advertising practices is located on the HUD's website. Federal credit unions must also comply with NCUA Rules and Regulations Section 701.31, 12 CFR Section 701.31.

**Non-Discrimination in Lending**

A credit union may not deny a loan or other financial assistance for the purpose of purchasing, constructing, improving, repairing, or maintaining a dwelling, nor may it discourage an application for such a loan, on the basis of the race, color, religion, handicap, familial status (having children under the age of 18), national origin, or sex of:

- The loan applicant or joint applicant
- Any person associated with the loan applicant or joint applicant
- The present or prospective owners, lessees, tenants, or occupants of other dwellings in the vicinity of the dwelling

It is unlawful to discriminate because of race, color, religion, handicap, familial status, national origin, or sex in determining the:

- Amount
- Interest rate
- Duration, or
- Other credit terms

Consideration of the following factors is not necessary to a federal credit union's business, generally has a discriminatory effect, and is therefore prohibited:

- Age or location of the dwelling
- Zip code of the applicant's current residence

- Previous home ownership
- Age or location of dwellings in the neighborhood of the subject dwelling
- Income level of residents in the neighborhood of the dwelling

A credit union may not rely on an appraisal that it knows or should know is based upon any prohibited bases or factors listed above.

**Legal Interpretations**

Because the FH Act was broadly written by Congress, the courts have ruled a wide variety of lending practices illegal under the Act, including some that the Act itself does not specifically mention but which the courts determined are illegal because they violate implicit requirements and prohibitions. Examples of some prohibited practices include:

- Redlining on a racial basis. "Redlining" is the practice of denying loans for housing in certain neighborhoods even though the individual applicant may be otherwise eligible for credit.
- Making excessively low appraisals in relation to purchase prices, based on prohibited considerations (closely akin to redlining).
- Discouraging applications for credit on prohibited bases, as well as outright denials. Taken together, the FH Act and ECOA produce a strong statutory prohibition against prescreening or discouraging applicants by housing sellers or lenders, even to the point of ensuring that their advertising policies do not have that effect.
- The use of excessively burdensome qualification standards for the purpose, or with the effect, of denying housing to protected applicants.
- Applying differing standards or procedures in administering foreclosures, late charges, penalties, or reinstatements, or other collection procedures.
- Racial notation or code on appraisal forms or loan forms (other than the information which §1002.13 of Regulation B requires the credit union to retain for monitoring purposes).
- Use by initial interview personnel of scripts designed to discourage protected applications.
- Patterns of significantly greater or exclusive use of insured or guaranteed loan programs by protected groups or in certain areas. This may indicate illegal "steering" to this type of lending by the credit union.

**Advertising**

Credit unions may not directly or indirectly engage in any form of advertising of real estate related loans that implies or suggests the credit union discriminates.

Any credit union that advertises real estate related loans must prominently indicate in the advertisement, in a manner appropriate to the advertising medium and format used,

that it makes such loans without regard to the prohibited bases. Additionally, every credit union engaged in real estate lending must provide a notice of nondiscrimination in its lobby and in each office where such loans are made. The notice must be clearly visible to the general public and must contain the Equal Housing Lender logo and language appearing in HUD's FH Act guidelines on advertising or NCUA Rules and Regulations Section 701.31(d)(3) for federal credit unions.

**Associated Risks**

The following risk areas apply to the compliance area:

- Compliance risk can occur when the credit union fails to implement the necessary controls to comply with the FH Act.
- Reputation risk can occur when the credit union receives negative publicity or declined membership confidence as a result of failure to comply with the FH Act.

**Additional Information**

Please refer to Section 701.31(e) of the NCUA Rules and Regulations for additional guidelines concerning nondiscrimination in lending. In addition, information is available on HUD's website at http://www.hud.gov.

Please note the ECOA and the Fair Housing Act should be read together in order to fully understand the scope of a credit union's fair lending obligations. For example, the bases of discrimination prohibited by the ECOA are similar, but not identical, to those prohibited by the FH Act.

# FAIR HOUSING ACT OPERATIONAL REQUIREMENTS

**Enforcement / Liability**

Administrative Enforcement Authority [Section 810 of the FH Act]

The U.S. Department of Housing and Urban Development (HUD) has responsibility for administrative enforcement for both federal and state-chartered credit unions.

Enforcement Mechanisms [Sections 810, 812, 813, and 814 of the FH Act]

The Attorney General may bring a civil court action directly when reasonable cause exists to believe persons or entities are engaged in a pattern or practice of FH Act violations. In addition, a person who claims to have been discriminated against may:

1) file a private civil action directly in federal court; or

2) file a complaint with HUD. HUD will investigate the complaint and it may attempt to resolve the grievance by means of conference, conciliation, and persuasion. If it finds a FH Act violation, HUD may take administrative action against the violator or, when reasonable cause exists to believe that persons or entities are engaged in a pattern or practice of violations, may refer the case to the Attorney General for action in federal court.

Penalties and Liabilities [Sections 812, 813, and 814 of the FH Act]

Administrative remedies available to HUD include permanent or temporary injunctions, restraining orders, or other relief including monetary damages and civil penalties. In civil court actions, the court may grant relief as it deems appropriate, including monetary damages, permanent or temporary injunctions, temporary restraining orders, or other similar remedy. Court-awarded monetary damages may include both punitive and actual damages.

It is unlawful to coerce, intimidate, threaten, or interfere with any person in the exercise of, or because they have exercised, rights granted by certain sections of FH Act [Section 818 of the FH Act].

# FAIR HOUSING ACT REVIEW CONSIDERATIONS

| Review Area | Requirements / Recommendations |
|---|---|
| Policies / Procedures | Ensure the policy for implementing FH Act does not tolerate prohibited discrimination in any aspect of a residential real estate-related transaction. |
| Nondiscrimination in Residential Lending | Ensure employees do not discriminate against any person in setting or exercising the terms or conditions of such a loan or discourage an application on the basis of race, color, religion, national origin, sex, handicap, or familial status (having children under the age of 18). <br><br> Note: The use of the term residential real estate-related transaction means (1) the making or purchasing of loans for the purchase, construction, improvement, repair, or maintenance of a dwelling secured by residential real estate or (2) the selling, brokering, or appraising of a dwelling. |
| Nondiscrimination in Appraisals | Do not rely on an appraisal of a dwelling if one knows or should know that the appraisal is based upon consideration of race, color, national origin, religion, sex, handicap, or familial status. <br><br> Do not rely upon an appraisal of a dwelling if one knows or should know that the appraisal is based upon consideration of a criterion which has the effect of discriminating on the basis of race, color, national origin, religion, sex, handicap, or familial status. <br><br> Do not rely upon an appraisal that one knows or should know is based upon consideration of any of the following |

|  |  |
|---|---|
|  | criteria, which generally have a discriminatory effect, and are not necessary to a federal credit union's business:<br><br>• The age or location of the dwelling<br>• The age or location of dwellings in the neighborhood of the dwelling<br>• The income level of the residents in the neighborhood of the dwelling<br><br>Note: See NCUA Rules and Regulations Section 701.31 regarding guidelines concerning possible exceptions or guidelines concerning the consideration of location factors. |
| Providing Appraisals | Creditors must provide a copy of the appraisal report used in connection with an application for credit to be secured by a lien on a dwelling. |
| Nondiscrimination in Advertising | Do not engage in any form of advertising of real estate-related loans that indicate the credit union discriminates on the basis of race, color, religion, national origin, sex, handicap, or familial status in violation of the FH Act.<br><br>Ensure advertisements do not contain any words, symbols, models, or other forms of communication that suggest a discriminatory preference or policy of exclusion in violation of the FH Act or the Equal Credit Opportunity Act.<br><br>Ensure real estate-related loan advertisements prominently indicate, in a manner appropriate to the advertising medium and format used, that the credit union makes such loans without regard to race, color, religion, national origin, sex, handicap, or familial status. (Federal credit unions see NCUA Rules and |

| | |
|---|---|
| | Regulations Section 701.31; state chartered credit unions see HUD guidance on advertising.) |
| HUD Regulations | Ensure compliance with all HUD regulations implementing the FH Act and NCUA Nondiscrimination regulations relating to residential real estate lending. (HUD regulations applicable to all credit unions are located at 24 CFR Parts 100, 103, and 110; and NCUA regulations applicable to federal credit unions are located at 12 CFR Section 701.31.) |
| Equal Housing Lender Poster | Display the Equal Housing Lender poster in the public lobby of the credit union and in the public area of each office where such loans are made, and it must be clearly visible to the general public. |
| Self-testing | Credit unions have a legal privilege in information developed as a result of self-tests that they would voluntarily conduct to determine their compliance with the FH Act. The privilege only applies if the definition of self-test is met and the credit union takes appropriate corrective action as described in the HUD implementing regulations, 24 CFR Part 100, Subpart C.<br><br>Note: Data or factual information that is available or can be derived from credit or application files is not privileged. Data collection required by law or any government authority is not a voluntary self-test. |
| Training | Provide training to all employees involved in any aspect of residential real estate, including the financing, selling, renting, advertising, brokering, and appraising of housing. All employees should be provided with training on the basic principles and core requirements of FH Act, along with other relevant fair lending laws and regulations. |
| Monitoring, Internal Review, Audit | Conduct periodic monitoring of the credit |

|  | union's compliance with the requirements of the FH Act, as well as other relevant fair lending laws and regulations. An internal or external audit should be conducted at least annually to assess overall compliance with the FH Act and to ensure the credit union's practices conform to its policies and procedures. |
| --- | --- |

# FAIR HOUSING ACT CHECKLIST

|  | Yes | No |
|---|---|---|
| 1. Does the credit union avoid the follow actions based on race, color, religion, sex, handicap, familial status, or national origin: [§805(a)] | | |
| • Refuse to make a mortgage loan | | |
| • Refuse to provide information regarding loans | | |
| • Impose different terms or conditions on a loan | | |
| • Discriminate in appraising property | | |
| • Refuse to purchase a loan | | |
| • Set different terms or conditions for purchasing a loan | | |
| 2. Does the credit union avoid any statements or advertisements that indicates a limitation or preference based on race, color, religion, sex, handicap, familial status, or national origin? | | |
| 3. Does the credit union include in its advertisements of real estate-related loans, that such loans are made without regard to race, color, religion, sex, handicap, familial status, or national origin? [§701.31(d)(1)] | | |
| 4. If the credit union makes real estate-related loans, does it display a notice of nondiscrimination in the public lobby of the credit union and in the public area of each office where such loans are made? [§701.31(d)(2)] | | |

# FAIR HOUSING ACT DEFINITIONS

**Definitions (Section 802)**

As used in this title (Title 42 of the United States Code)

### *Secretary*
The Secretary of Housing and Urban Development.

### *Dwelling*
Any building, structure, or portion thereof which is occupied as, or designed or intended for occupancy as, a residence by one or more families, and any vacant land which is offered for sale or lease for the construction or location thereon of any such building, structure, or portion thereof.

### *Family*
Includes a single individual.

### *Person*
Includes one or more individuals, corporations, partnerships, associations, labor organizations, legal representatives, mutual companies, joint-stock companies, trusts, unincorporated organizations, trustees, trustees in cases under Title 11 of the United States Code, receivers, and fiduciaries.

### *To rent*
Includes to lease, to sublease, to let and otherwise to grant for a consideration the right to occupy premises not owned by the occupant.

### *Discriminatory housing practice*
An act that is unlawful under Section 3604, 3605, 3606, or 3617 of this title.

### *State*
Any of the several States, the District of Columbia, the Commonwealth of Puerto Rico, or any of the territories and possessions of the United States.

### *Handicap*
with respect to a person-
(1) a physical or mental impairment which substantially limits one or more of such person's major life activities,
(2) a record of having such an impairment, or

(3) being regarded as having such an impairment, but such term does not include current, illegal use of or addiction to a controlled substance (as defined in Section 802 of Title 21 of the United States Code).

### *Aggrieved person*
Includes any person who-
(1) claims to have been injured by a discriminatory housing practice; or
(2) believes that such person will be injured by a discriminatory housing practice that is about to occur.

### *Complainant*
The person (including the Secretary) who files a complaint under Section 3610 of this title.

### *Familial status*
One or more individuals (who have not attained the age of 18 years) being domiciled with-
(1) a parent or another person having legal custody of such individual or individuals; or
(2) the designee of such parent or other person having such custody, with the written permission of such parent or other person.

The protections afforded against discrimination on the basis of familial status shall apply to any person who is pregnant or is in the process of securing legal custody of any individual who has not attained the age of 18 years.

### *Conciliation*
The attempted resolution of issues raised by a complaint, or by the investigation of such complaint, through informal negotiations involving the aggrieved person, the respondent, and the Secretary.

### *Conciliation agreement*
A written agreement setting forth the resolution of the issues in conciliation.

### *Respondent*
(1) the person or other entity accused in a complaint of an unfair housing practice; and
(2) any other person or entity identified in the course of investigation and notified as required with respect to respondents so identified under Section 3610(a) of this title.

### *Prevailing party*
Has the same meaning as such term has in Section 1988 of this title.

Office of Consumer Financial Protection and Access
National Credit Union Administration

# HOME MORTGAGE DISCLOSURE ACT (REGULATION C) OVERVIEW

The Home Mortgage Disclosure Act (HMDA), implemented by Regulation C (12 CFR 1003), requires financial institutions, including credit unions, to compile and disclose data about home purchase loans, home improvement loans, and refinancings that it originates or purchases, or for which it receives applications. Data to be recorded on reportable transactions include:

- Application or loan number
- Date application received
- Loan type
- Property type
- Purpose
- Owner occupancy status
- Loan amount
- Request for preapproval
- Type of action taken and date
- Property location (by metropolitan statistical area, state, county, and census tract)
- Applicant information (ethnicity, race, sex, and gross annual income)
- Type of purchaser of loan
- Reasons for denial (optional)
- Rate spread (effective January 1, 2004)
- Home Ownership and Equity Protection Act of 1994 (HOEPA) status (effective January 1, 2004)
- Lien status

The purpose of Regulation C is to provide the public with data that can be used to:

- Help determine whether credit unions are serving the housing needs of their communities
- Assist public officials in distributing public-sector investments so as to attract private investment to areas where it is needed
- Assist in identifying possible discriminatory lending patterns and enforcing compliance with anti-discrimination statutes

Regulation C is not intended to encourage unsound lending practices or the allocation of credit.

### Exempt Institutions

A credit union is exempt from the requirements of the regulation for a given calendar year if on the preceding December 31st:

- It had neither a home office nor a branch office in a metropolitan statistical area (MSA) or
- Total assets were at or below the threshold established by the Consumer Financial Protection Bureau (CFPB) or
- It made no first-lien home purchase loans (including refinancings of home purchase loans) on one-to-four family dwellings in the preceding calendar year.

The CFPB adjusts the asset threshold based on the year-to-year change in the average of the Consumer Price Index for Urban Wage Earners and Clerical Workers, not seasonally adjusted, for each twelve-month period ending in November, with rounding to the nearest million. NCUA notifies credit unions about the asset threshold change each year in a Regulatory Alert.

### Disclosure and Reporting

A non-exempt credit union must maintain a loan/application register (LAR) on which it will enter data about each application received and each loan originated and purchased. The credit union must send the LAR to NCUA HMDA Processing (done by the Federal Reserve Board on behalf of the Federal Financial Institutions Examination Council (FFIEC)) by March 1st following the calendar year for which loan data is compiled.

Using data from the LAR, the FFIEC will prepare and send to the credit union a series of tables that will comprise the public mortgage loan disclosure statement for that credit union. The credit union must make its disclosure statement available to the public at its home office no later than three business days after receiving it. In addition, if a credit union has branch offices in other MSAs, it must make the disclosure statement available using one of two options:

- It can make the disclosure statement available in at least one office in each of those MSAs, within ten business days of receipt from the FFIEC or
- It can send a copy of the disclosure statement if someone makes a written request, within fifteen calendar days of receiving the request. If the credit union chooses this option, it must post the address for requesting copies in each branch office in an MSA.

The disclosure statements need only contain data relating to the metropolitan statistical area for which the request is made.

**Enforcement**

The CFPB enforces compliance with HMDA for all credit unions with greater than $10 billion in assets.

NCUA enforces compliance with HMDA for all credit unions with less than $10 billion in assets. NCUA may impose administrative sanctions, including civil money penalties for repeated failure to file or late filing. NCUA does not consider an error in compiling or recording required data a violation of the regulation if it was unintentional and occurred despite the credit union's maintenance of procedures reasonably adapted to avoid such errors. NCUA's policy has been to require credit unions to correct and resubmit their HMDA data when a HMDA LAR validation conducted during an onsite fair lending examination reveals sample error rates exceeding certain thresholds or errors making analysis of a credit union's data unreliable. Credit unions are required to correct and resubmit HMDA data when 10 percent or more of the HMDA LAR sample entries contain errors or when an individual data field contains an error rate of 5 percent or more.

**Associated Risks**

- Compliance risk can occur when the credit union fails to implement the necessary controls to comply with HMDA.
- Reputation risk can occur when the credit union incurs fines and penalties as a result of the failure to comply with HMDA or poor publicity as a result of negative trends displayed by the disclosure statement.
- Strategic risk can occur when the credit union fails to perform adequate planning and due diligence in regard to HMDA.

**Additional Information**

Credit unions engaged in mortgage lending should obtain the publication: *A Guide to HMDA Reporting: Getting it Right!* It can be downloaded from the FFIEC website at https://www.ffiec.gov/hmda/guide.htm.

# HOME MORTGAGE DISCLOSURE ACT (REGULATION C) OPERATIONAL REQUIREMENTS

**Disclosures / Notices**

Modified Loan Application Register (LAR) [Sections 1003.5(c) and (d)]

A lender must make its LAR available for public inspection upon request after modifying it to protect the privacy interest of applicants and borrowers by deleting the:

- Application or loan number
- Date of receipt of the application
- Date of action taken

The modified LAR must be available following the calendar year for which the data relates, no later than March $31^{st}$ for requests received on or before March $1^{st}$ and within 30 days for requests received after March $1^{st}$. The modified register need only contain data relating to the metropolitan statistical area (MSA) for which the request is made. The lender must make its modified register available for a three year period.

Mortgage Loan Disclosure Statement [Section 1003.5(b)]

The disclosure statement, prepared by the Federal Financial Institutions Examination Council (FFIEC), must be made available to the public for inspection and copying at the lender's home office within three business days after receiving it from the FFIEC.

In addition, a lender must do either one of the following:

- Make the statement available in at least one office in each additional MSA where it has offices within ten business days of receipt from the FFIEC or
- Post the address for sending written requests for the statement in the lobby of each branch office in an MSA where it has offices, and mail or deliver a copy of the statement within fifteen calendar days of receipt of a written request.

The lender must make the disclosure statement available to the public for a five year period.

Lobby Notice [Section 1003.5(e)]

The lender must post a general notice about the availability of its HMDA data in the lobby of its home office and of each branch office located in an MSA.

**Recordkeeping**

Record Retention [Section 1003.5]

A copy of the Loan Application Register (LAR) must be retained for a period of at least three years.

The modified LAR must be available to the public for a period of three years.

The disclosure statement must be available to the public for a period of five years.

**Reports**

Reporting Requirements [Section 1003.5(a)]

A credit union must submit its complete loan application register (LAR) by March 1st following the calendar year for which the loan data is compiled to the Federal Reserve Board.

**Enforcement / Liability**

Administrative Enforcement Authority

The CFPB enforces compliance with HMDA for all credit unions with greater than $10 billion in assets. NCUA enforces compliance with HMDA for all credit unions with less than $10 billion in assets.

Penalties and Liabilities

Administrative sanctions, including civil money penalties, may result from violations of the regulation.

# HOME MORTGAGE DISCLOSURE ACT (REGULATION C) REVIEW CONSIDERATIONS

| Review Area | Requirements / Recommendations |
| --- | --- |
| General Coverage | Determine whether the credit union is subject to the requirements of HMDA / Regulation C.<br><br>Credit unions are exempt from reporting requirements for a given year if on the preceding December 31$^{st}$:<br><br>• The credit union did not have a home or branch office in an MSA or<br>• The credit union's total assets were at or below the asset threshold or<br>• The credit union did not make a first lien home purchase loan (or refinancing) on a one-to-four family dwelling in the preceding calendar year. |
| Policies / Procedures | Ensure policy and procedures for implementing HMDA are in place for collecting and maintaining accurate data of covered loans and applications. |
| Collection of Data | Compile data on applications for, and originations and purchases of, home purchase loan, home improvement loans, and refinancings.<br><br>The required information must be retained on a loan application register (LAR) in the format prescribed in Appendix A to Regulation C. |
| Data on Ethnicity, Race, Sex, and Income | Ensure information on ethnicity, race, and sex is collected in the manner prescribed in Appendix B to Regulation C.<br><br>If the applicant chooses not to provide this |

|  |  |
|---|---|
|  | information for an application taken in person, the lender must note this fact on the form and note the data based on visual observation or surname, to the extent possible.<br><br>If the applicant chooses not to provide this information for an application taken by mail, Internet, or telephone, the data need not be provided.<br><br>Ethnicity, race, sex, and income data may but need not be collected for loans purchased by the credit union. |
| Excluded Data | Ensure certain transactions are excluded from being reported, including:<br><br>- Loans made or purchased in a fiduciary capacity<br>- Loans on unimproved land<br>- Construction and temporary financing loans<br>- Purchase of an interest in a mortgage pool<br>- Purchase of servicing rights<br>- Loans originated prior to the current reporting year and acquired as part of a merger or acquisition |
| Reporting Requirements | Submit the completed HMDA LAR to the Federal Reserve Board by March 1$^{st}$ following the calendar year for which loan data is compiled. |
| Modified Loan Application Register | Ensure the modified register is made available to the public after removing the following information: application or loan number, date the application was received, and date of action taken. |
| Disclosure Statements | Ensure the disclosure statement prepared by the FFIEC is made available to the public for inspection and copying at its home office within three business days of receipt from the FFIEC. |

|  |  | If a credit union has branches in other MSAs, it must make disclosure statements available using one of two options (see Overview section). |
| --- | --- | --- |
| Lobby Notice |  | Post a general notice regarding availability of HMDA data in the lobby of its home office and each branch office located in an MSA. |
| Training |  | Provide training to employees whose duties are impacted by HMDA. |
| Monitoring |  | Ensure collection of data for the HMDA LAR is being properly recorded within the required timeframes. |

# HOME MORTGAGE DISCLOSURE ACT CHECKLIST

|  | Yes | No |
|---|---|---|

1. Did the federally insured credit union originate, in the preceding calendar year, at least one home purchase loan or refinancing of a home purchase loan secured by a first lien on a one-to-four family dwelling? [§1003.2]

2. Did the federally insured credit union have a home or branch office in a Metropolitan Statistical Area (MSA) on December 31$^{st}$ of the preceding year? [§1003.2)]

3. Did the federally insured credit union's total assets exceed the established threshold as of December 31$^{st}$ of the preceding year? [§1003.2] Note: The Consumer Financial Protection Bureau adjusts the asset threshold annually.

If you answered "Yes" to <u>all</u> three questions, the federally insured credit union is subject to HMDA and the remainder of the checklist should be completed.

If you answered "No" to <u>any</u> of the three questions, the federally insured credit is exempt from HMDA for the year in question.

4. Is the credit union ensuring data regarding applications for, and originations and purchases of, home purchase loans, home improvement loans, and refinancings for each calendar year are properly compiled? [§1003.4(a)]

5. Does the credit union maintain the necessary records to compile the required data?

6. Is there an adequate audit trail to test the accuracy of the data compiled?

7. Is accurate census tract information (2010 census data) available for the compilation of data?

8. Are loan/application registers (LARs) completed fully and accurately? [§1003.4(a) and Appendix A]

9. Is the credit union properly collecting data on ethnicity,

race, sex, and income? [§1003.4(b) and Appendix B]

If an applicant chooses not to provide information, for applications taken in person, on ethnicity, race, or sex, is this fact noted on the form and is this data noted, based on visual observation or surname, to the extent possible? [§1003.4(b) and Appendix B]

10. Does the credit union avoid reporting data on transactions excluded by the regulation? [§1003.4(d)]

11. If the credit union reports 26 or more entries, is the credit union submitting data in an automated, machine readable, and conforming format no later than March 1st following the calendar year for which data was compiled? [§1003.5(a) and Appendix A]

If the credit union reports 25 or fewer entries on their HMDA LAR and submits reports in paper form, does the credit union submit two copies that are typed or computer printed in the proper format?

12. Are applications and loans recorded on the credit union's LAR within 30 calendar days after the end of the calendar quarter in which final action is taken? [§1003.4(a) and Appendix A]

13. Is the disclosure statement prepared by the FFIEC made available to the public at the credit union's home office no later than 3 business days after receiving it from the FFIEC? [§1003.5(b)(2)]

14. Is the disclosure statement made available to the public, within ten business days of receiving it, in at least one branch office in each other metropolitan statistical area (MSA) where the credit union has offices? [§1003.5(b)(3)(i)] **or**

Does the credit union post the address for sending written requests in the lobby of each branch office in other MSAs where the credit union has offices, and mail or deliver a copy of the disclosure statement within fifteen calendar days of receiving a written request? [§1003.5(b)(3)(ii)]

15. Does the credit union make its modified loan application

register available to the public after removing the application or loan date, the date the application was received, and the date action was taken? [§1003.5(c)] _____ _____

16. Are the disclosure statements and modified registers available to anyone for inspection and copying during normal public business hours? [§1003.5(d)] _____ _____

17. Are disclosure statements made available to the public for five years and modified registers made available to the public for three years? [§1003.5(d)] _____ _____

18. Has the credit union posted a general notice about the availability of its HMDA data in the lobby of its home office and of each branch office located in an MSA? [§1003.5(e)] _____ _____

19. Are policies, procedures, and training adequate to ensure compliance with HMDA? _____ _____

20. Does management ensure that affected personnel are aware of the requirements of HMDA? _____ _____

# HOME MORTGAGE DISCLOSURE ACT (REGULATION C) DEFINITIONS

**Definitions (Section 1003.2)**

### *Application*
(1) In general, an application means an oral or written request for a home purchase loan, a home improvement loan, or a refinancing that is made in accordance with procedures used by a financial institution for the type of credit requested.

(2) Preapproval programs - A request for preapproval for a home purchase loan is an application under paragraph (1) if the request is reviewed under a program in which the financial institution, after a comprehensive analysis of the creditworthiness of the applicant, issues a written commitment to the applicant valid for a designated period of time to extend a home purchase loan up to a specified amount. The written commitment may not be subject to conditions other than:

(i) Conditions that require the identification of a suitable property;
(ii) Conditions that require that no material change has occurred in the applicant's financial condition or creditworthiness prior to closing; and
(iii) Limited conditions that are not related to the financial condition or creditworthiness of the applicant that the lender ordinarily attaches to a traditional home mortgage application (such as certification of a clear termite inspection).

### *Branch office*
(1) Any office of a bank, savings association, or credit union that is approved as a branch by a federal or state supervisory agency[1], but excludes free-standing electronic terminals such as automated teller machines; and
(2) Any office of a for-profit mortgage-lending institution (other than a bank, savings association, or credit union) that takes applications from the public for home purchase loans, home improvement loans, or refinancings.

### *Dwelling*
Residential structure (whether or not attached to real property) located in a state of the United States of America, the District of Columbia, or the Commonwealth of Puerto

---

[1] There is no law or regulation that requires NCUA approve credit union branch offices established within the United States, and NCUA does not issue such approvals. Accordingly, a domestic credit union branch office may qualify as a HMDA branch office without approval by a federal or state regulatory agency

Rico. The term includes an individual condominium unit, cooperative unit, or mobile or manufactured home.

### *Financial institution*
(1) A bank, savings association, or credit union that:

(i) On the preceding December 31$^{st}$ had assets in excess of the asset threshold established and

published annually by the Consumer Financial Protection Bureau for coverage by the act, based on the year-to-year change in the average of the Consumer Price Index for Urban Wage Earners and Clerical Workers, not seasonally adjusted, for each twelve-month period ending in November, with rounding to the nearest million;

(ii) On the preceding December 31$^{st}$, had a home or branch office in a metropolitan statistical area (MSA);

(iii) In the preceding calendar year, originated at least one home purchase loan or refinancing of a home purchase loan, secured by a first lien on a one-to-four family dwelling; and

(iv) Meets one or more of the following three criteria:

(A) The institution is federally insured or regulated;

(B) The mortgage loan referred to in paragraph (iii) of this section was insured, guaranteed, or supplemented by a federal agency; or

(C) The mortgage loan referred to in paragraph (iii) of this section was intended by the institution for sale to Fannie Mae or Freddie Mac.

Note: The definition of "financial institution" also includes other provisions covering types of institutions that are not credit unions.

### *Home-equity line of credit*
Open-end credit plan secured by a dwelling as defined in Regulation Z (Truth in Lending), 12 CFR Part 1026.

### *Home improvement loan*
(1) A loan secured by a lien on a dwelling that is for the purpose, in whole or in part, of repairing, rehabilitating, remodeling, or improving a dwelling or the real property on which it is located; and

(2) A non-dwelling secured loan that is for the purpose, in whole or in part, of repairing, rehabilitating, remodeling, or improving a dwelling or the real property on which it is located, and that is classified by the financial institution as a home improvement loan.

### *Home purchase loan*
A loan secured by and made for the purpose of purchasing a dwelling.

### *Manufactured home*
Any residential structure as defined under regulations of the U.S. Department of Housing and Urban Development establishing manufactured home construction and safety standards (24 CFR 3280.2).

### *Metropolitan statistical area*
A metropolitan statistical area as defined by the U.S. Office of Management and Budget.

### *Refinancing*
A new obligation that satisfies and replaces an existing obligation by the same borrower, in which:

(1) For coverage purposes, the existing obligation is a home purchase loan (as determined by the lender, for example, by reference to available documents; or as stated by the applicant), and both the existing obligation and the new obligation are secured by first liens on dwellings; and

(2) For reporting purposes, both the existing obligation and the new obligation are secured by liens on dwellings.

### Additional Information

For more information and clarification regarding definitions of terms used, refer to the publication: *A Guide to HMDA Reporting: Getting it Right!* It can be downloaded from the FFIEC website at https://www.ffiec.gov/hmda/guide.htm.

www.ingramcontent.com/pod-product-compliance
Lightning Source LLC
Chambersburg PA
CBHW062124220526
45471CB00010B/3870